ANCIENT GREECE

The Greatest Civilization

THE HISTORY HOUR

HISTORY

CONTENTS

PART III
EARLY CLASSIC GREECE

PART IV
THE PERSIANS

PART V
GRECO-ROMAN AND BYZANTINE GREECE

PART VI
Conclusion

PART VII
Further reading

❄ I ❄

INTRODUCTION

❧

The very first democracy in the world found its origins in Ancient Greece. The most exquisite art and architecture of the world had its origins there. While education had its roots in many cultures after the Bronze Age, education found its flowering in the rise of some of greatest literature ever written. From the very small country of Greece came the development of the higher sciences. Even the most celebrated of sports events, the Olympics, started in a small city-state of Athens. Many governmental buildings to today are lined with columns embellished on top with designs created in Greece. The Doric column was named after the Dorians, one of the root races indigenous to Ancient Greece. The Ionic column was named after their satellite colony, Iona in current-day Turkey. The Corinthian column is named after the ancient city of Corinth on the Southeastern coast of Greece. Live theater entertainment originated in the amphitheaters of Ancient Greece. Nowhere in the civilized world can anyone find no element from this civilization of explorers of the mind and the mysteries of myth. Greece has a history that lies within the experience of everyone.

❧ II ❧
WARS AND OMENS
OF MORE

❦

Dawn comes slowly when the light is low. The age of passing from darkness into the light is punctuated by mystery, omens and mounting terror as new and fragile populations of Asia Minor migrated toward the great Mediterranean Sea. Full of fish and rich black earth ready for harvest, the Mediterranean brought a new life to them. The Greeks built fine cities of stone hewn from the earth to honor their deities – only to have them destroyed by earthquakes, natural disasters and then each other.

❦

Initially, Greece was a world silent to history until writing came into being, revealing a luxury of belief and wealth of culture and art.

SUDDENLY THEY WERE GONE: COLLAPSE OF THE MINOANS AND MYCENAEANS

An ancient stone hearth staunchly stands against the wall at the base of the stairs. Broken pottery lies upon mounds of ash and pumice. The ashes roll down the steps in the wind. Faded frescoes of maidens and warriors on chariots still decorate the once beautiful walls. Fleets of ships are depicted with all their riggings, children picking flowers, fishers carrying home their catches. And outside there are valleys under blankets of ash. Bases of stone pillars poke out. White gypsum rocks reach toward the sky.

Gone are the brave bull leapers – those agile lads who somersaulted over wild bulls at the grand arena in Crete. The harbors and coves are covered in ash and broken stone. The huge pottery containers were left behind – too heavy to be taken by people fleeing for their lives.

The eruption at Thera in 1646 BC was as powerful as 40 atomic bombs, but that wasn't the only one. Some of the people from the outskirts of the island and on Crete could read the signs and departed on their ships in great haste. Some fled to the land of the Hittites (present-day Turkey) and a few other families to mainland Greece.

They had script carved on tablets called *Linear B*. Some inscriptions were indecipherable. There are no human remains there; no doubt swept away from the great tsunami that followed.

It was the end of the Bronze Age. It was the absolute end of the Minoan and Mycenaean Civilizations. After that, came the darkness.

THE SILENCE OF THE
DARK AGES

❧

The people no longer had their syllabi, and nothing to use for writing or reading. The instinct for survival was all they had. They organized themselves by families called *oikoi*. It was an extended family from which descended generations that followed. Families bonded closely together, having been through the earthly disasters. Each family unit spoke its own dialect, but it was a form of Greek. Outsiders were called *barbaroi*, meaning one who doesn't speak Greek. That term became corrupted to mean "*barbarian*."

❧

There were no tribes then, as the populations were spread about. Only later, there were clans called *genose*. Even later some *genose* united to form tribes. The people in the village – *demos* – were interrelated. They lived together and fought against invaders. Some boys who could afford armor and weapons joined military clubs and were trained in the "**reli-gious art**" of war. They fought under to command of a *basileus,* who was the commander.

⚜

The land was fertile. The Greeks grew flax and wheat and raised livestock. Most had their little plots of land. However, there were the lost ones who had no land of their own, nor the skill to earn their way as warriors. These landless, poverty-stricken men were called *thetes*.

⚜

Homer, in his epic the *Odyssey,* related how the legendary king, King Odysseus told his son, Telemachus, about a *thete* he had with him a swineherd by the name of Eumaeus:

⚜

> *"...Of wide Crete he avows him to be by lineage, and he says that round many cities of mortals he has wandered at adventure. Now, as a runaway from a ship of the Thesprotians, has he come to me, and I will give him to thee for thy man (manservant); do with him as you wilt."*

⚜

The *thetes* were the lowest class in the society of the Dark Ages in Greece. However, most people besides the *thetes* were poor and primitive in their understanding and intellectual development.

THE "BIG MAN"

ⵛⵯⵛ

S ome men in Greece – and indeed in Melanesia and Polynesia – were considered wise men among whom was chosen a chief who one was charismatic. He could attract many followers. As the people gave him gifts, he could become rich. However, the wealth he accumulated was used to humanistic purposes – the protection of his clan and economic support for it at times of great need. His upward mobility to become a ***big man*** was usually based on merit and his willingness to take on responsibility. The "Big Man" was also obliged to trade with other "Big men" in other clans to maintain peace and order.

AGORA

An ***agora*** was a meeting. Decisions among the people in the clan were cursorily democratic. Most of the issues that arose were about decisions to go to war with another community or not. Decisions that were made were made by shouting approval or disapproval. If the topic was war, only the soldiers met. In cases where clans or villages met, usually, the lowest classes weren't expected to attend.

THE IRON AGE

The bronze that the Greeks made from 3000-1200 BC was useful for weapons and shields, but it bent. That made it increasingly less effective in battle. Different cultures developed the smelting of iron at different times. Between the years 1300-1200 BC – the Iron Age and the Dark Ages of Greece – iron was the most common metal used, although tin and copper were utilized for different purposes like the manufacture of utensils. Tin, however, started to become scarce and those who could not acquire copper had to resort to clay or metal alloys. The people who emigrated from Crete and who lived on the mainland in Greece traveled, though only occasionally, and came into contact with the Hittite civilization in Asia Minor, and learned from them. In addition, there were some nebulous travelers on the Mediterranean called *sea people*," who brought with them news of the accomplishments of other civilizations. It is also possible that the sea people who may have settled in small colonies on mainland Greece taught those techniques to the Greek clans.

PROTOGEOMETRIC ART STYLE

❦

While digging themselves out of the Dark Ages, the tribal primitives were reviving their culture from times past. At that time, the art was a co-mixture, as it was influenced by newer tribal legions with different styles. No longer did it resemble the beautiful ornate painted patterns of highly costumed people on their amphora. The designs were geometric in the form of bands, squares, and circles.

❦

Red Clay was plentiful in the area and mined in the bogs. The three-firing technique was used to create the pottery. The process:

- A shape is formed on a pottery wheel, then placed in a kiln – an oven that was brought to a temperature of about 900° Celsius. That took about 8 hours. If extra oxygen is supplied, the vessel turns red.

- The oxygen supply is then reduced, and the red gets darker. Usually, green wood was used to block air inlets, which will reduce the oxygen content.
- The full intake of oxygen is restored.
- The object is thoroughly cooled and ready for use.

The colors on these vases, plates and drinking vessels were created by different oxidizing procedures performed on certain areas of the pot. Deprivation of oxygen or **"*sealing*"** creates a darker or even black shape.

LACONIA

Southern Greece, called Peloponnese, was the most politically active area of the peninsula. It was divided into six major regions:

- Messina
- Arcadia
- Achaea
- Elis
- Argolis
- Corinth

Through Laconia flows the Eurotas River. Along that river lay the major city-state of Sparta. To the right of Peloponnese, across the water, on the Southeastern coast of Greece lay Attica, the region that contained the capital, Athens.

THE MYTHOLOGICAL DORUS OF
THE DORIANS

The alluring green-blue sea nymph, **Orseis** arose from the Ionian Sea, west of Peloponnese and mated with **Hellen** (a male). *Hellen* is considered the first ancestor of the Hellenes, or Hellenistic Greeks. His progeny begot three branches of Greeks on the mainland:

- Aeolus (the Aeolians)
- Xuthus (the Achaeans and Ionians)
- Dorus (the Dorians)

Dorus and his descendants, the Dorians, made their homes in Central Greece just North of Delphi and Mount Parnassus – a majestic limestone mountain where King Odysseus was gored in his thigh while on a boar hunt – as related in Homer's **Odyssey**. Dorus allied himself with **Heracles**, son

of the great god, **Zeus** himself. In Rome, he was called
Hercules.

of the great god, **Zeus** himself. In Rome, he was called
Hercules.

DORIANS: THE PEOPLE OF THE GIFT

⚜

After the Minoans and Mycenaeans abandoned Crete after the disasters, the Dorians came in. ***Heracles*** gave these people a gift to hold for his (Heracles) descendants. They were charged with guarding that inheritance for his descendants until they could pass the gift along to the next generation.

⚜

The Doric dialect of Greek was spoken in Crete, Peloponnese, the islands in the Aegean Sea and even some further colonies – "***Magna Graecia***" in Southern Italy and the city of Syracuse in Sicily. Some Doric dialects appeared in Asia Minor as well.

⚜

Both the Spartans and the Athenians shared the attributes and dialects of the Doric people after intermarriage of the two people.

THE OLYMPICS 776 BC TO THE PRESENT

⚜

The Olympic Games originated in Greece in the 8th Century BC. The Olympics celebrate their head deity, **Zeus**. This was a time of ancient barbeques and challenging competitions among the athletes of the day. Many competitions were combat-related, and a few were fought to the death. Even wars were held in abeyance during the Olympics. In fact, that was one of the laws passed by Lycurgus of Sparta (see below). Early events included running, jumping, discus throwing, foot races, chariot racing, wrestling, boxing, equestrian events, and the "***pankration***." Pankration was like a boxing-wrestling match with no rules except prohibitions against biting and gouging the opponent's eyes out!

⚜

- Some of the other requirements:
- Every athlete is naked

- In pankration and wrestling, the competitors are covered with oil
- Boxers were forbidden to attack male genitalia
- False starts in races were strictly forbidden and offenders are given corporal punishment for doing so
- There are no points awarded and no weight classifications in this form of boxing (!)

Heracles (**Hercules**, as he was called in Rome) was the mythical king of Laconia and son of **Heracles** himself. The daughter of **Heracles** was Princess Sparta, and the famous city-state is named after her and her family. Another version of the myth gives the name "**Lacedaemon**."

LYCURGUS OF SPARTA

ʊ♥ʊ

Lycurgus was a legend and a lawgiver. Not too much is known of the dates when he lived, admits the ancient and famous biographer, Plutarch when he said,

> *"A man cannot speak anything at all of Lycurgus, who made the laws of Lacedaemonians, but he shall find great contrarity of him amongst the historiographers...And yet they agree worst about the time he lived in."*

Plutarch himself indicates that Lycurgus was descended from the deity, **Hercules** (Heracles), himself.

ʊ♥ʊ

Lycurgus established laws regarding distribution of land among the Spartans:

- a bicameral body of representatives consisting of 28 men with voting rights
- a currency that only applied to Sparta in an effort to promote internal trade
- a *"**mess hall**,"* which operated much like a pot-luck supper to which everyone brought a dish
- military residential schools for young boys
- a suspension of all wars and conflicts during the Olympic games

SOCIAL CLASSES

The Spartans conquered and controlled the indigent population and there were basically three classes in the society:

- the royal houses
- the Spartan military establishment
- the helots.

The Spartan military were the warriors and lived with their families. They also controlled the politics of the area. The helots comprised the lowest class, and they were the agricultural workers.

SPARTAN ROYALTY

The government was a diarchy, meaning it consisted of two hereditary kings. During the periods prior to factual written history, mythology blended with reality. For example, those hereditary kings were considered priests of **Zeus.** They were at the head of a council of elders.

THE SPARTAN MILITARY
ESTABLISHMENT

Elders were all male and were between the ages of 28-60+ years of age, serving in their capacity as leaders for life. Beneath them was a council of citizens who met in a people's assembly. An executive committee was composed of five members, chosen by lot and they served for just one year. All of them were called *"citizens,"* and were trained in the martial arts and politics. Homosexuality was a common practice in the course of their societal/military training.

Women of this class were more fortunate than even women of the middle ages. They could own and inherit property and even engage in military activities. When many of the males died in the regional wars, their wives inherited their property, and soon women owned more property in Sparta than the men.

HELOTS

Helots were those who were farmers. They provided for themselves, their families, the military families and, of course, the royal families. Occasionally they could rise in status when the military forces recruited them.

THE SPARTAN WARRIOR

The Spartan warriors weren't a separate social class, *per se*. Military service among males was compulsory. At the age of 60, they could retire from military service but remained on call for the remainder of their lives. The well-trained Spartan warrior was called a **hoplite**. These were the heavily armored infantry. For weapons, they used wooden spears and short swords called **xiphos**. Each warrior also carried a dagger. Their helmets and breastplates were made of bronze. Even though this was the iron ages, bronze is a more pliable metal.

The warriors moved in formations called Phalanxes, which means they march side-by-side in two divisions – the right flank and the left. They played music and often let out war cries when the enemy came close. The fighting was mostly hand-to-hand. Usually, they preceded each battle with a sacrifice.

FIGHT TO DEATH IF YOU MUST

❦

The code under which Spartans fought was cold and harsh. According to the ancient writer-poet, Tyrtaeus, who reportedly was from Sparta in Laconia:

"Fight in a stubborn, close array, my boys!
Feel your anger swell. There is no place
In combat for love of life.
We must fight to the death for our land and children, giving
No thought to lengthening life."

❦

In the first verse above, note the use of tightly formatted troops. **(phalanxes)**

MESSENIA (AKA MESSINI)

❦

Like Laconia, Messenia was also an agricultural region, and the tribes there raised livestock. Basic products were sold to the neighboring areas and consisted of olives, figs, and raisins. Meat, milk, cheese and fish were also consumed. These people built great amphitheaters in which they staged plays and musical shows.

FIRST MESSENIAN WAR
743-724 BC

☙

The Spartans and Messenians did cooperate on occasion for economic purposes, but enmities often broke out. Each area secretly craved dominance over the territory of the other. This war, so the ancient history texts relate, was provoked by continual incidents of cattle theft. By way of example, one time, an athlete, Polychares of Messenia, leased some property from Euaiphonos, a Spartan herdsman. However, he stole some cattle from the herdsman and immediately sold them. When Euaiphonos discovered that, he demanded that the son of Polychares go with him to help him recover the cattle or monetary compensation for them. After the boy went with him, Euaiphonos murdered the boy. Once Polychares discovered that, he tried to get the judges of the region to resolve this issue. When they didn't, Polchares swore revenge on Spartans and initiated a killing spree. That, in turn, triggered feud-like slaughters. This accelerated to the point that the Messenians were at war with the Spartans.

Overwhelming greed triggered further warfare. Once the Spartans saw the farms and ranches of the Messenians, they desired them. Although they engaged in initial conflicts, the Messenians didn't want a full-flung war with Sparta, as the Spartans were superior warriors. The people of both regions didn't want their country torn apart and appealed to the kings. King Polydorus of Sparta then proposed distributing some of the unused lands in Messenia to the people of the regions. After some time, this solution was insufficient, and the hatred accelerated. King Alcmenes of Sparta then assembled an army and swore not to stop warring until they were satisfied. The non-fighters among the population fled to the temples or outside the province. Spartan soldiers sacked the cities of Messenia. When the Messenians went up against them, King Euphaes directed them to attack brutally in a frontal assault. This was ineffective against the strong 8-man deep phalanxes, and they had to retreat numerous times until they were forced to retreat to Mount Ithome. Roads leading to the 3,000' high summit were zigzagged. The fortress atop was flatter ground, which was natural to the area. There was a great city wall there built of solidly cemented white stone.

Oracles, or soothsayers, were often consulted before battles or when there was a vital issue at stake. The Oracle at Delphi (see later in the Chapter) was the best known. After the first Messenian War, one of the generals approached the Oracle about it would be advantageous to continue the war.

The Oracle then told the supplicant to relate to the king that a royal virgin must be sacrificed. This was done in a bloody sacrifice upon the altar at Delphi. The unfortunate victim was the daughter of a Messenian hero by the name of Aristodemus. After that, the Spartans held off for a number of years. That was a customary delay in wartime right through the Late Middle Ages.

SECOND MESSENIAN WAR
685-668 BC

꧁꧂

As the helots, who were the slave-farmers, increased in population, they needed new territory on which to raise their families and provide food for their overlords, the Spartans. They rebelled and invaded Laconia and confiscated some of the lands of the Spartans. Under their leader, Aristomenes, they won the initial battles and occupied some of Laconia. During the course of a counter-attack, however, the Spartans captured Aristomenes and imprisoned him. Later, Aristomenes escaped and reconnoitered the troops. Then the Messenians moved into Mount Elra and made several raids to more surrounding Spartan land.

꧁꧂

Ten years later, Sparta again attacked and captured as many of the Messenians as they could, putting them back into slavery. The writer-poet Tyrtaeus himself was a warrior (as were all males in Spartan society). He himself fought in the Second Messenian War. He related the account of taking the Messenians in battle:

> *"Like overloaded, worn-out mules, they bring their masters,*
> *by painful compulsion, half of everything their fields*
> *produce...men and their wives, mourning their master*
> *whenever one was overtaken by death."*

Then the lyric poets of that ancient century praise the victorious warriors by describing their courage in battle:

> *"In war, no man is good unless he faces blood and death,*
> *taking a stand in enemy reach. That is excellence; that is*
> *the noblest contest a young man can win. The city and all*
> *of its people gain when a man takes an unflinching stand*
> *in battle, gives no thought to flight but calmly wages life*
> *and spirit with a cheerful word to the soldier beside him.*
> *In war, that is a 'good man.'"*

THE FALL OF MESSENIA

⚘

After the years' long delay, the Spartans themselves consulted the Oracle of Delphi. Although the exact advice is unknown, she predicted that the Spartans would be successful − the direct antithesis of her earlier prophecy. They invaded with their light infantry forces using their traditional phalanxes and overcame the Messenians. The Messenians who did not escape to neighboring city-states became helots. The Spartans then became the landowners and divided up some of the land among them to build farms and temples. The helots were charged with working the land.

THE ORACLE AT DELPHI

⚙

It was customary to consult with the gods when at war, so the Messenians sent out a messenger to the Oracle of Delphi. It was the religious custom of both enemies to delay until the consultation was made. The **"Oracle of Delphi"** was a priestess of the order. The most famous oracle was Pythia. She had a collection of priests around her and served at the shrine of **Apollo.** She would first be presented with the issue, and then go through a period of fasting, after which she fell into a deep sleep in her chamber, which was deep into the rocks there. There was an underground spring there that would feed into a pool deep in the earth. It was served by a spring – the Castalian Spring.

⚙

According to the ancient legends, there were fissures in the earth above the underground spring. Above one of the fissures, the people had built a tripod throne. It was from that throne; the Delphi would give the prophesies and instructions while under a trance. The whole ceremony was cloaked in an aura of mystery.

A number of science teams had explored the Delphi region and ascended from the pits with varying explanations. Although most investigators indicated that there were no fissures, the legends don't match the facts. However, geological history has shown that there were a number of earthquakes and ground instability in the past, indicating the possibility that there may have been and may even still be fissures somewhere in the array of tunnels under the mount.

One investigative team under De Boer discovered evidence for these fissures and located springs with pools. The scientists initially found just calcite deposits which would result in producing the "trance-like" conditions ancient writers described, but the trance wouldn't be very strong. Further investigations, though, revealed that deep within the earth, the Delphi site had a bituminous deposit that is high in the emission of hydrocarbons and pitch. Vaporization of the fumes from this area yields a high level of ethylene gas. On mixtures of close to 20%, it can bring about hallucinations and euphoria. These states can also cause alterations on one's voice and make a person scream. Clinicians have concluded that people can seem to speak logically, depending upon the dosage inhaled. The dosage alternated with the passage of time depending upon whether or not there were recent tremors. So, there is some evidence to the descriptions given in the ancient texts.

ARCHAIC ATHENS 800-440 BC

❧

Athens was the capital and major city-state of Southeastern Greece called Attica. This area was controlled by nine *archons* or administrators. The assembly of the people, called Ekklesia, contained all member of the society. The lowest class were called the Thetes. Many of the city-states in Greece at that time were run by tyrants. They came from Attica or even areas in Asia Minor.

❧

The very ancient Linear Script B that was used during the Mycene period ceased after the volcanic explosions. In the years following 1100 BC, the Greek people adopted the alphabet of the Phoenicians from Asia Minor. The Greek language was further advanced during successive centuries, making it the much easier for scholars to determine historical events. Of course, there were always religious myths inter-woven with history. That was based on a need to justify oneself and was a reason to unite as a culture. It was a means of security and identity that united people. In addition, biases were always present, depending upon the writer and his nationality. Other random biases and even contradictory statements were made by a number of writers who were re-recording events that were told from the viewpoints of participants who wouldn't necessarily be aware of the entire scope of an event or battle.

ATHENA

❧

Every notable city-state of the archaic times needed a divine god or goddess with whom to identify. Athens was named after the goddess, **Athena**. She was the divine entity of handicraft, warfare, and wisdom. She was called **Minerva** in the Roman tradition.

❧

The myth in which she is ensconced is the story of **Athena's** birth. She was said to have emerged from the head of **Zeus**, her divine father. Her stories are intertwined with those of other deities such as the heroes **Perseus**, **Jason** and **Heracles.**

❧

According to one of the greatest Greek philosophers, Plato, **Athena** was intelligent and had the mind of a god. She knew many things that mere mortals and even lesser gods didn't know.

☙❧

In her role as "***Athena Promachos***," she led soldiers into battle. The battles she sponsored were those that were for a just cause. Athena was a virgin and worshipped at the festivals of Pamboeotia and Panathenaea. Silver coins with her head embossed on it, Athenian tetradrachm, were worth four drachmas each.

☙❧

About Athens, the first leader of Athens, Solon, solemnly spoke the praises of its great goddess, ***Athena***:

> *"Our city will never perish by decree of Zeus*
> *or whim of the immortals; such*
> *is the great-hearted protector, child of thunder, who holds*
> *her hands above us: Athena."*

☙❧

Solon also related to his people some of the values of being an Athenian who for a lifetime lives the qualities of her wisdom:

> *"A man who owned silver and gold in abundance,*
> *acres of wheat-bearing land,*
> *horses and mules is no richer than one whose belly,*
> *sides and feet are well,*
> *who sometimes enjoys a boy or woman and lives*
> *in harmony with his age."*

SOLON OF ATHENS

※

Solon was the first most prominent personage in Athens and lived from about 638-558 BC. Although he was of noble birth, he wasn't a wealthy noble, and therefore, it is only known that he was admired by many. Solon was an accomplished ancient poet, and it's possible that people admired him because of his verses.

※

When he came into power, there were a number of issues in the city-state. The basic theme of them was rivalry – Ideological and economic rivalry; regional rivalry; and rivalry between clans.

※

Ideological and Economic rivalry – Athens was initially an oligarchy, meaning that it was ruled by the "**rich and** *powerful*." Wealth in terms of gold and currency, as well as land ownership, determined the class into which someone was born or achieved. The poor and landless virtually worked like lease-holders of farms, and some were paid a pittance for their products. If the poor couldn't pay their leases, they were thrown in debtors' prisons.

⚜

Regional Rivalry – the rivalry of the Spartans and Messenians is an example of regional rivalries. Jealousy, need, and greed resulted in conflicts and the victorious in those conflicts confiscated all or part of the lands of the others. As for those on the losing side (who survived the battles), they became the new slaves or thetes.

⚜

The rivalry between Clans – Clans, as seen in the Dark Ages, were composed of many extended families who had united together within the bond of heredity and kinship. They were often subdivided within by members of a clan considered to be wealthier, and classes of aristocrats were thus created.

⚜

In time, Solon became bloated with his own wealth, enjoyed his increasing power, and transformed into a hated tyrant. Before he reached that stage, however, Solon put introduced far-reaching reforms to Athens. The first had to do with class status.

NEW SOCIAL CLASSES

U nlike the during the era of the tyrants, the social classes were subdivided based upon income and land. The city was run by archons, but there were also treasurers who functioned on an equal plane. Basically, the top down structure was:

Pentacosiomedimnoi

- 9 archons and treasurers
- Council of Areopagus (elders who met on the prominent rock called the Areopagus)
- Council of 400 (prominent citizens who were in charge of daily affairs), also called "*boule*."
- Ekklesia (the popular assembly)

Hippeis

- Cavalry who had at least 300 medimnoi (currency measure) of income. They were comparable to the ***"upper middle class."***

❦

Zeugitae aka Hoplites

- Those with lands that could produce 200 medimnoi of dry or wet goods per year. Those men could also serve in the army.

❦

Members of the Zeugitae were eligible to run on a council of 500 which was election-based, as well as run for lower offices. Later on, in 457 BC, a member of the zeugitae could run for archon, the top office.

❦

Thetes

- As in earlier days, the Thetes were the lowest class of citizens
- Unlike in the earlier days, however, they could partake in the Ekklesia or the popular assembly.

HELIAIA – THE COURT

⁂

The heliaia consisted of 6,000 members who were chosen by lot for juries. They were male citizens age 30 or over. If one was in debt, or being punished for a civil crime, they were ineligible. Jury members served for one year and were called *"heliasts"* when serving in that function.

⁂

Persons who headed up the court were the archons themselves or lesser officials. Crimes heard in those courts could be criminal or civil and there was a process for appeal.

⁂

According to the ancient historian, Plutarch, by establishing this new stratum:

> *"...he (Solon) pleased neither party, but the rich were dissatisfied at the loss of their securities, and the poor were still more so because the land was not divided afresh, as they hoped it would be, and because he...had not established absolute equality."*

❧

Solon spoke of his social changes, realizing that they may not satisfy everyone, especially the wealthy:

> *"I gave the people the rights they needed without stealing or adding honor. Thanks to my precautions, the powerful and wealthy suffered no disgrace. I lent both sides my shield's protection, conceding to neither an unjust victory."*
>
> *"The people follow those leaders best who neither tolerate license nor oppress. When men of bad character prosper greatly, satisfaction turns to arrogance."*

FIRST PERSIAN WAR 492-490 BC

৩৵৩

The Greek city-states had satellite settlements in Anatolia (current-day Turkey), which was part of the vast Persian Empire under King Darius I. Ionia was one of them. The city-states of Eretria and Athens supported the territory called Ionia in Asia Minor and battled the Persians over control of it. King Darius of Persia was a vengeful tyrant who was determined to take full control of Iona and wanted to take out Athens for its insolence over Iona. In preparation for battle, King Darius prayed to the great god, **Zeus**,

> *"Zeus, I pray that it may be granted me to take vengeance upon Athens!"*

THE BATTLE OF MARATHON
490 BC

In the poem by the same name, which was the most monumental battle of the First Persian campaign, Elizabeth Barrett Browning wrote:

"The Persians rose, and crowd th' embattled plain,
and stretch their warlike millions to the main;
And now th' Athenians throng the fatal field,
By fame inspired, and swords and bucklers wield;
In air sublime their floating banners rise,
The lances blaze, the trumpets rend the skies.
And then Militias: 'Athenians, hear,
Behold the Persians on the field appear,
Dreadful in arms; remember, Greek, your fame,
Rush to the war, and vindicate your name;
Forward! Till low in death the Persians lie,
For freedom triumph or for freedom die.'"

As a result of this Greek victory, the Persians pulled back but did manage to gain control of the Aegean Sea.

53

THE ACROPOLIS 490-488 BC

છ🙪૭

It was on the mount Acropolis that the Athenians constructed their temple to honor ***Athena***, who saved their land. ***Athena*** was their patron deity. The most famous of the buildings there, the Parthenon, overlooks the magnificent city. A statue of ***Athena***, called ***Athena Polias***, was in the center of the Parthenon, and its columns were adorned with statues of all the other sacred deities of Greece. This structure was built and rebuilt through the years due to the destruction that occurred during many wars. The Parthenon was built on two massive limestone platforms and surrounded by 6-12 columns carved in the Doric style. The style of the Parthenon as seen today is much larger than the original and has many more elaborately decorated columns.

THE SECOND PERSIAN WAR
480-479 BC

❦

In 480 BC, before the Parthenon and more minor temples and shrines could be completed upon the hill of the Acropolis, the Persians raged in. With their axes and clubs, they absolutely destroyed the original Parthenon. Then they sacked the city, sending its inhabitants fleeing to the hills and surrounding countryside.

❦

There was even a smaller wooden statue of Athena there, part of which survived and was discovered by archeologists.

❦

King Darius also craved mastery of Sparta, as well as Athens, according to ancient historian, Herodotus. If the Persians could control Athens and Sparta, two of Greece's prime city-states, that would provide a gateway into Europe proper.

Athens, in particular, was the most accomplished city-state in the Mediterranean World, with its highly intellectual scholars, beautiful white-stoned buildings and temples, and elaborate tapestries and ornate artifacts.

56

ॐ

King Darius I died before he could conduct the entire Second Persian War, but was followed by his heir, Xerxes, who was likewise determined to seek revenge against Greece for their resounding victory in the First Persian War.

THE ORACLE AT DELPHI
PREDICTS THE BATTLE

꧁꧂

Tismenus, an athlete from Elias, another Greek area in Laconia often performed well in athletic contests. Yet it was said that he was a prophet of sorts. According to the histories of the ancient Herodotus, Tismenus consulted the Oracle who predicted great victories for him. Tismenus naturally thought that her prediction referred to his upcoming Olympic games, so he practiced very intensely. The Oracle also told him he must be declared a citizen of Sparta in order to win these victories. When he approached Sparta with the request, they dismissed him, even though they knew of his reputation as both an athlete and a potential prophet.

꧁꧂

However, when the Spartans were under severe threat from the Persians who were preparing to invade them, it occurred to them that the Delphi's reference to ***great victories*** for

Tismenus may refer to victories in battle, not the Olympic games. According to Herodotus:

> *"This Tisamenus the Elian became a Spartan – in quality of a seer, took part with them in five signal victories. The first of which was that at Plataea – next that at Dipaea, over all the Arcadians, except the Mantineans; then that over the Messenians, at the Isthmus."*

THE BATTLE OF PLATAEA 479 BC

❧

This battle was one of the most significant battles in the Greco-Persian War. It took place on the Southeastern peninsula of Greece where Athens is located. Sparta, Tegea and Messene are on the Southwestern peninsula, and those city-states were all allied with other city-states against Commander Mardonius of the Persians. The Greek allies were overwhelmingly outnumbered. The Persians boasted of nearly 300,000 men while the Greek allies were just 50,000. The outlook for a Greek victory looked dim, despite the Oracle's prediction.

❧

Midway through the battle, the beloved city of Athens was already standing in ruins, but the Athenians were known for their determination and their willingness to fight until no man is left standing. As a means of avoiding a continuation of the fight, Commander Mardonius made an offer of peace in exchange for control of Athens, promising them a degree of self-governance. Mardonius attempted to use the arguments of superior troop strength to persuade the Greeks to lay down their arms. Alexander I, the Greek King of Macedon at the head of the Greek peninsula, presented his answer in the name of the Greek allies including Athens and Sparta:

> *"The degree to which we are put in the shadow by the Medes' (Persians') strength is hardly something you need to bring to our attention. We are already well aware of it. But even so, such is our love of liberty, that we will never surrender."*

⚜

Although there were a few further skirmishes during the second phase of the battle, the Greeks had occupied the higher ground and wouldn't be lured to come down to wage an all-out fight. Both sides hesitated and were at a basic standstill for as long as 11 days. The Greek commanders depended upon divine omens and tried to predict the outcome were they to descend from the hills. Omens from the readings of animal entrails weren't good, so the Greek forces were told to hold back. Finally, Pausanias, the Greek general, received a positive omen from the gods. He then had his soldiers descend the highlands and rush headlong into the Persian phalanxes. Although the Greeks were still using bronze spears which were easily broken, they switched to their trusty swords and hacked away at the Persians, who lacked strong armor themselves. It was a bloody battle, but the Tegeans and Athenians battled incessantly. Then a bold Spartan soldier reached down on the ground, picked up a heavy stone, leaped on the horse of the Persian Commander, Mardonius, and thrust the rock at his head. Mardonius was immediately killed. With a much smaller force, the Greeks won and gave chase to the Persians who retreated North and West, back to their lands in Asia Minor. They had never seen such a power that could overcome overwhelming odds. Greece was perceived as being favored by the gods.

AGRICULTURE AND ECONOMY
OF ARCHAIC GREECE

※

Eighty-percent of the arable land in Greece was devoted to agriculture. Wheat and barley were their most commonly-produced staples. Corn, lentils, garlic, cabbage, beans, onions and chickpeas also supplemented their vegetables. There were olive tree orchards used to produce olive oil which formed the liquid oil that could be used as a binding agent once mixed with ground up powdered grains. It could be made into a primitive leavening agent using just warm water and wheat flour by letting the mixture sit in warmth with a wet cloth top. Hence, the coming of ancient Greek flatbreads. This early form of flatbread was somewhat harder than pita bread but was the foundation for further improvement of this staple which is still enjoyed today across the world.

※

Figs, pears, grapes, apples and almonds were also cultivated. Once they had invented writing, the Greek wrote books about agriculture and harvesting in the proper seasons. For example, this extract from the ancient Greek poems of Hesiod about harvesting corn demonstrates the combination of a "***how-to***" book with a lovely poem:

"Forget not, when Orion first appears,
To make your servants thresh the sacred ears;
Upon the level floor the harvest lay,
Where a soft gale may blow the chaff away;
Then, of your labor to compute the gain,
Before you fill the vessels, mete the grain.
Sweep up the chaff, to make your work complete;
The chaff, and straw, the ox and mule will eat."

The constellation, Orion, first appears in November in the Northern Hemisphere. Ancient people usually used the constellations to determine seasons, and there were a lot of similar comparisons made between astronomy and the agricultural cycles.

Animals raised in Greece included of goats, sheep and traditional farm animals with the exception of cows and cattle. The terrain was generally too rocky and mountainous for them. Some oxen were raised to use for plowing and pulling wagons. Horses were also kept, but most were raised by the aristocrats and used for equestrian events and warfare.

Beekeeping was a regular practice. The Greeks used the honey to sweeten their foods because there were no other sources for sucrose in Greece at the time.

FISHING

Although one might think that fishing was a major industry in ancient and archaic Greece, it wasn't. The waters of the Eastern Mediterranean are saltier than that in other places. Unlike the oceans, very little plankton can survive there, depleting a natural food source for medium and small fish. However, large fish like sharks, rays, mackerel, tuna, and swordfish could be fished there. Much fish had to be imported from other countries along the Mediterranean, making it necessary to preserve the fish they purchased from Italy and other countries in salt.

TRADE

Trade along the countries in the Aegean Sea to the East of Greece flourished during ancient and archaic periods. Anatolia was located at the end of many of caravan routes from the Far East, so an oriental influence was seen even in Greek art of the period. Egypt was also very accessible to them, so the rich textiles from there poured in.

ART

During the Dark Ages, the Protogeometric style prevailed (see earlier), but as trade grew the oriental styles came in and now complex human figures – mostly of warriors – adorned their vases and drinking vessels. Greece was notable for action-packed figures mostly painted in black. When the red clay was developed, the black figures against the red were striking. Using their hardening techniques, sometimes red figures on black appeared. Those were the more elegant masterful pieces seen in the homes of the royal family and the wealthy.

❧ III ❧

EARLY CLASSIC GREECE

One of the greatest of Greek philosophers, Plato, wrote his **Dialogues**. In Book VIII of the **Dialogues**, a cycle of successive unjust constitutions was discussed and reflects the evolution of the Greek society throughout the ages. Those periods are:

- Timocracy
- Oligarchy
- Democracy
- Tyranny

Timocracy refers to an epoch featured by a government ruled by the property owners. Oligarchy refers to a period when the state is run by a select few composed of the wealthy. Democracy is the era in which the citizens rule. Tyranny is characterized by the rule of one. This alteration of governing style was a grim assessment. The most notable solution for ending this depressing cycle lies in the improvement of men in terms of their innate sense of justice and goodness. Greece evolved through all these different periods, but Classical Greece had supreme achievements that outshined the inferiorities of its government. Classical Greece was a period of art and intellectual thought that was manifest in its magnificent buildings and enviable bodies of learning that flowed, despite its shortcomings. What was good and true in the human being led to the development of a country that scholars study to this day. The Classical period displayed the best and the worst in human nature.

THE PELOPONNESIAN LEAGUE
505 BC

❂

Sparta was the most powerful of the Southern city-states in Greece, and united with local city-states to protect themselves not only against the Persians, but against Athens. The members of the Peloponnesian League:

- Sparta
- Corinth
- Melos
- Mantinea
- Elis

❂

Each paid dues and owed allegiance to the rest if one of its members was attacked.

THE DELIAN LEAGUE 478 BC

To ward off any revenge attacks from the Persians, the city of Athens formed the Delian League. Although city-state membership shifted from time to time during the years, this league generally included:

- Athens
- Aegina on the Eastern coast
- Byzantium in Anatolia
- Argos
- Megara
- Boetia (including Thebes)
- Argives (islands)
- Mantinea

FIRST PELOPONNESIAN WAR
460-445 BC

ealousy between Sparta and Athens erupted when Athens started constructing giant long city walls, and Sparta was vehemently opposed to that. They had enjoyed a period of peace with Athens and saw these fortifications as a threat. Athens also wanted to expand its territory on mainland Greece. Athens had a formidable naval fleet – one that made it powerful in controlling trade and activity on the Mediterranean Sea. Sparta objected to Athens extra-Grecian alliances, including that with Inarus, a Libyan who controlled part of Egypt. Athens befriended Inarus because the new Persian king, Artaxerxes, attacked him. Therefore, they had a brief alliance with Egypt. Several theaters of the Peloponnesian War broke out including the island of Cyprus and Phoenicia. If Athens and the Delian League prevailed, that would aid in the establishment of an Athenian hegemony. As the Spartans developed conspiratorial theories against Athens because of this alliance, they became suspicious that the Athenians were attempting to undermine Spartan power. It was a correct assumption. To avoid an Athenian victory, Sparta engaged them and their Peloponnesian League at Tangara in Central Greece.

74

suspicious that the Athenians were attempting to undermine Spartan power. It was a correct assumption. To avoid an Athenian victory, Sparta engaged them and their Peloponnesian League at Tangara in Central Greece.

BATTLE OF TANGARA 457 BC

The Athenian forces confronted the Peloponnesian League in the city-state of Boetia. According to the mutual defense agreements under the Delian League, the city-states of Argos and Megara aided Athens. These were huge forces: 14,000 under the Delian League and 11,500 for Sparta's Peloponnesian League. Because the Athenians controlled the sea and had the support of Megara in the mountainous regions, Sparta lured them on to the plains of Tangara, where they roundly defeated them. Athens' dream of hegemony in Greece then faded until the second phase of the Peloponnesian War fought years later.

PERICLES: THE GOLDEN AGE
461-429 BC

෴

As Sparta had suspected, Athens became the most prominent power in all of Greece, despite their losses. Politically, Athens was divided between two political parties: the democrats or populists and the conservatives. Pericles was a populist who rose to the leadership of Athens after conflicts with the conservative, Cimon, from one of the wealthy families of Athens.

෴

Pericles decrees aided the poor and lowered the property taxes for all. He paid wages to the jurymen who belonged to the Heliaia court. Freedom of expression was permitted. Democracy flourished in Athens.

THE ACROPOLIS
RECONSTRUCTED 437 BC

❧

After the Persians had virtually destroyed their sacred temples, including the Parthenon, Pericles ambitiously started rebuilding it under the management of Phidias. A grand pillared entrance of many marble steps lined with marble colonnades formed the Propylaea, which was the grand entrance to the Parthenon. For those projects, Pericles obtained financing through the Delian League. There were four wings in each of the four directions with stone gateways for the entry of worshippers. Thus, due to the efforts of Pericles, the Parthenon greets thousands of tourists today coming to admire a magnificent building constructed in Ancient Greece.

⬥

Every major town and city had theaters in which plays were performed in great amphitheaters. Pericles wanted all his people to be well-educated, so he permitted the poor to attend free of charge.

⬥

One of the most famous plays of the Fifth Century was **Agamemnon,** a story about King Atreus of Mycenae's murder and the foe, Paris from Troy who abducted Helen, the wife of Menelaus, Atreus' brother-in-law. That event set off the Trojan War. This was also the topic of Homer's **Iliad** and **Odyssey**. Aeschylus, who wrote **Agamemnon** said:

> *"Ten years have come and gone since when*
> *The two great chiefs of Atreus' race,*
> *Ordained of Jove and Kings of men,*
> *A royal paid in power and place,*

Marshaled their thousand ships and more..."

❧

Note in the above-quoted verse, the reference to the immense naval superiority of Athens – "*...**their thousand ships**.*"

❧

The famous playwright, Sophocles, wrote **Antigone** in 441 BC, where the story of King Oedipus of Thebes who unknowingly marries his own mother, Jocasta is told. That gave rise to the term "**Oedipus Complex**," in Freud's dream interpretation referring to a theorized love created by a sexual desire for the mother and hatred of the competition, that is, the father.

THE SECOND PELOPONNESIAN
WAR 431-404 BC

&0&

The peace held out after the First Peloponnesian War until one of the small colonies of Athens on the island of Sicily went to war with Syracuse. Two little Athenian city-states, Segesta and Leontine, were at war, and asked Athens for assistance. Although there were skirmishes between them, that appeal was a ruse created so that the Athenian colonies could gain more control of Sicily and some borderlands in Italy itself. Athens still had a desire for hegemony over the Mediterranean World.

BATTLE OF SYRACUSE 415-413 BC

吊

A huge fleet of Athenian ships was sent to Sicily, hoping to get added support from the small settlements along the Italian coast for this venture. No one wanted to join in. The Athenians had sent in ten ships to Syracuse, but the Athenians were forced to conduct warfare on land and had very little by way of land forces. Syracuse, in the other hand, had an accomplished cavalry and united with Sparta as an ally. A cavalry encounter wouldn't work for the Athenians, so they sent in a double agent to falsely inform the soldiers of Syracuse that the Athenians were on the way to the city-state of Catana, which lay further East. While the Syracusans and Spartans were diverting to Catana, The Athenians boarded their vessels and sailed South and then into the harbor just West of the city of Syracuse. With their allies, the Argives and the Mantineans and other allies, the Athenians entered Syracuse, built a fort, and situated themselves in such a way that they were protected by slopes on their left and the sea on their right. When the Syracusans and Spartans arrived, they went into their traditional flank positions of eight deep, with their cavalry to one side provided the backup force. Head-on the Athenian hoplites and the Syracusans clashed. Syracuse and the Spartan troops fell back and tried to escape over a river, but the Athenians had destroyed the bridge.

Although the Athenians could have occupied the temple of **Zeus** on the high ground, their commander, Nicias, avoided that based on religious grounds. That was a mistake. He also had the opportunity to besiege the city itself but didn't do so and decided to retire to Catana until the battle could be re-engaged when Spring came. That was another mistake. In the year 413 BC, Athens was defeated, and lost nearly all its soldiers.

Still hopeful for a counter-attack, Nicias made plans to do so. However, the Greeks during the Classical Period were still committed to depending very heavily upon omens in order to select the best times to do battle. When there was an eclipse of the moon, the Athenians hesitated and waited. Then Nicias planned to escape out to sea. Out in the harbor at that point, there were huge warships called triremes that had three layers of hundreds of rowers who could use their weapons against the smaller Athenian vessels. The Athenians let out to sea but failed. Of the hoplites who were still on land, they had to march a number of days to reach a friendly city. A daylong bombardment was launched by the Syracusans and Spartans, and the Athenians were forced to surrender to

Glyippus of Syracuse. That meant that Sparta now controlled Sicily and Athens as well. The war was over. Athens wasn't destined to lead the Mediterranean World.

RULE OF THE THIRTY TYRANTS
404 BC

꧁

As a result of their victory, Sparta enforced a tyrannical oligarchical rule upon Athens. "*Oligarchy*" means a rule by the elite. For a period of eight months, these thirty individuals were the interim government. Democracy as the Athenians understood it was virtually eliminated. Anyone who spoke out against this government was executed. Sparta imposed a strict code of law and appointed 3,000 loyal citizens to enforce it. Those men were armed. The Thirty Tyrants executed anyone whom they considered disloyal to the state without the benefit of a trial. Corruption was also rampant among the oligarchs because they often executed men in order to confiscate their lands. Violence and collusion were rampant. The estimate of people executed was 1,500. Many more Athenians were exiled.

THE RISE OF SPARTA

After their successful victory in the Peloponnesian War, Sparta became like an empire in Southern Greece. They had destroyed the Athenian vessels, and with it, the Athenian mastery over the sea. Then Sparta built its own fleet of military and merchant ships. The society had a solid, rigid caste system in place. Boys, from the age of five and up, received firm military training. Sometimes, it was cruel. The military schools were isolated from the rest of society and were entirely male. Homosexuality was encouraged regardless of personal sexual preference. Young boys slept in the open and had to care for themselves – to "**live off the land**," if you will. Courage in battle wasn't considered a virtue; it was a requirement. And it went to extremes. At the age of twenty, boys were inducted into "mess units," which were like battalions. If one wasn't inducted by the other members into one of those units, they were forced to become members of a lower caste. If anyone showed the least sign of fear in battle or in the mock battles they held for practice, they were demoted into "inferior" regiments and called insulting names like "***tremblers***."

☙❧

Members of these elite groups of warriors were called "***Similars***." They all had plots of land on which to farm. Helot-serfs would work the farms and were bound to that land, rather than to the men running it.

GOVERNMENTAL STRUCTURE

⁂

There were two hereditary kings. Their obligation was to serve as religious officials and as field marshals in battle. Next were the Ephors, who were overseers. The Ephors were advised by a body of twenty-eight elders. They were elected by an assembly of Similars. There were frequent conflicts between the roles of kings versus the roles of Ephors, as the job descriptions were vague. Often it depended upon the personalities of either. This, in turn, led to political rivalries that resulted in opposing and changeable sets of regulations. Occasionally these differences caused a deadlock in policies or in violence.

⁂

The Apella was the citizens' assembly. Decisions were made by shouting, and sessions were loud and disorganized. Every Similar had the duty to attend.

The Helots were the lowest caste and consisted of people from the lands conquered by Sparta over the years. Many came from Messina in the Peloponnese. They are bound to the land like slaves and even served in the military. The Helots represented a perennial threat to Sparta, and the Similars had to guard against possible insurrections by them. The Similars utilized a mysterious group of secret assassins called the **Krypteia** who were assigned to assassinate rebellious Helots or trouble-makers. Sometimes, Helots were killed simply because they were good-looking and had a noble look. The primary motive was to keep the Helots in a state of fear.

SOCRATES AND HIS TRIAL 399 BC

❧

Socrates was the penultimate philosopher who lived during this tumultuous age. His method of teaching was called the "**Socratic Method**," or "**Elenchus**," and seeks insight into the truth by a series of questions. This was a "**dialectic**," or dialogue, by which the student learns through answering and posing questions in order to arrive closer to the truth. Thought processes used are logic, analysis, and critical thinking. It is a thought process enforced upon someone who either makes a statement about a belief or a conclusion made from their experience. An interlocutor than follows up by a series of questions. Here is an example of Socratic thinking, analyzed according to Socrates' method:

❧

First, the **topic/issue** is presented:

> *"People from different cultures than the mainstream culture feel alienated."*

⁕

Second comes such **oppositional** questions as:

> *"What makes you believe that about someone?"*
> *"Does that happen to everyone who comes from different cultures?"*
> *"Can you tell they feel alienated?" "How?"*
> *"Does everyone feel alienated at one time or another?"*

⁕

Third, questions might be asked related to the **implications and consequences:**

> *"Are there symptoms of feeling alienated?"*
> *"Are you talking about young people?"*
> *"Are you implying that they shouldn't be here?"*
> *"What happens if someone feels alienated?"*
> *"Is it bad to feel alienated?"*
> *"Should alienation be overcome?"*

⁕

Fourth, the **evidence, the support and the motives** for the issue:

> *"How do you know they are alienated?"*
> *"Do you think they might always feel that way no matter where they are?"*

"*What happens if someone feels alienated?*"
"*If they feel alienated, why do you think they feel that way?*"
"*What should be done if someone feels alienated?*"

THE TRIAL OF SOCRATES

৩৯৫

S ocrates was perceived as a philosopher who threatened the rigid structure of the government. In the year 399 BC, Socrates was accused of:

- Impiety
- Inventing new gods
- Corrupting the youth

৩৯৫

There is no written account of Socrates' exact words at his trial. He taught verbally only. His devoted student, Plato, wrote about Socrates' defense in his treatise, **Apology**. The term "**Apology**" used in this sense doesn't mean begging forgiveness; it means a defense.

৩৯৫

Regarding the first charge, *"impiety,"* Socrates questioned the prosecutor, Anytus, as to what he meant by *"impiety."* According to Plato, Anytus couldn't present a clear definition of *"impiety"* to start with.

As for the second charge, *"inventing new gods,"* Socrates asked for evidence. None was presented.

As for the third charge, *"corrupting the youth,"* he cross-examined Meletus, who was the man who brought the charges into court. Again, there were no witnesses nor evidence of such.

Socrates was tried and executed for political reasons. Athens during Pericles' reign had been firmly rooted in democracy. Socrates was anti-democratic because he questioned whether that system would yield competent leadership. Too many diverse opinions would be involved, and the *"truth"* couldn't be the product of popularity. He preferred governments that were led by a learned few who had weighed and studied issues and demonstrated competence and experience. That, however, wasn't appropriate for Athens under the constraints of Spartan dominance. Sparta didn't favor independent thinking. So, when Socrates, in his lessons, objected to tyrannical leaders who made unjust decisions based on fallacious justifications, that offended their Spartan overlords.

Socrates also objected to the choice of leaders or others with weighty decisions (like members of his own jury) being made by the casting of lots. His arguments against selecting people for governmental or other important positions, he felt, should be based on the degree of wisdom and right thinking they were capable of. Socrates once used the argument that if people wanted to hire a flute player, they wouldn't select him by casting lots. They would select him for his skills. Thus, Socrates objected to the radical society that was in place at the time of his trial.

⚜

Socrates' critics, on the other hand, were confused. Because Socrates also didn't favor an open democracy like that of old Athens, his critics thought he was advocating a Spartan-style of rule like that of the thirty tyrants. That wasn't his intention either, so his accusers tried to condemn him on "***guilt by association***." One of his former students, Critias, was a member of the thirty tyrants. In fact, Socrates – along with four others – were ordered to bring a man named Leon of Salamis, before the court for the execution, and Socrates was being tested for his loyalty. When Socrates refused to bring Leon in for execution, he was questioned. In response, he said:

> *"...I gave all my attention to avoiding doing anything unjust or unholy. Powerful as it was, that government did not terrify me into doing a wrong action. When we came out of the rotunda, the other four went to Salamis and arrested Leon, but I simply went home."*

⚜

He strove to help his students learn how to think critically and render conclusions that were true and just objectively. Despite their demonstration of loyalty, some of Socrates' associates had also been condemned for their independent thinking – and one was executed – because he suggested that changes be made in the system.

❧

When he was asked to renounce his philosophy and abandon his teachings, Socrates refused. Hence, he was sentenced to death by imbibing hemlock, a poison.

SUICIDE?

Some commentators have indicated that Socrates committed suicide by failing to renounce his philosophy and beliefs. However, Socrates was firmly rooted in his convictions. Were he to renounce his beliefs, he would be demonstrating that his beliefs meant nothing. What kind of example would that leave if a man who claims to have a belief in seeking the universal truth, but isn't willing to die for that belief?

Socrates firmly held to the process he advocated that taught others a process for thinking that can be applied even today. He is noted for saying:

"The unexamined life is not worth living."

THE FALL OF SPARTA 371 BC

❧

As the Similars became more powerful, they worked themselves up into a higher class of elites. As competition for land increased, many of the Similars, in addition to the elites, became wealthy landowners. However, there were other Similars who weren't quite so successful and were relegated to lower levels of society because they couldn't pay their annual dues.

❧

The Peloponnesian Wars had taken its toll on the Similars also, as many of them fell in battle. That made it necessary to force more Helots to become warriors. Class warfare prevailed. The rich landowners spent a great deal of time feasting and celebrating. Drunkenness was becoming more common. Ambitious Similars, on the other hand, broke treaties and made war on city-states with whom they had been at peace. Provinces lying outside their territories were also attacked and anti-Spartan forces formed within those areas.

⛬

Loyalty had been the backbone of unity in Sparta. However, it was weakening. During the reign of King Agesilaus II (398-358 BC), the King conducted a divining session – a traditional practice among leaders. The omens were bad, and the sooth-sayer predicted that there would be *"a most terrible"* conspiracy against the rule of the Spartan king.

⛬

There really was a conspiracy and it unraveled shortly thereafter. In the Spartan territory of Laconia, a brilliant military commander by the name of Cinadon, was a Similar who ambitiously desired more wealth and power. An informant approached the Euphors, saying that this man – Cinadon – had organized a plot for 40 Spartans to perform a coup d'état against the government.

⛬

The Euphors then sent out false orders that Cinadon be dispatched in his military capacity to go out to the frontier regions in Messenia. The Euphors then ordered a small unit and a cavalry force to go after Cinadon. After a brutal interrogation, Cinadon revealed the names of his co-conspirators. All were arrested and put to death.

BATTLE AGAINST THEBES 394 BC

The Spartan Empire had to constantly defend its conquered territory. King Agesilaus had to take a huge army of hoplites (foot soldiers) to the city-state of Thebes and faced their warriors head-on. Although he did win, the Spartan King, Agesilaus, was wounded and lost 350 more of his skilled hoplite men.

THE BATTLE AGAINST THRACE
390 BC

❧

The Athenians, still anxious to overthrow their Spartan overlords, moved to assist the city-state of Thrace against the Spartan adversaries. Sparta was now becoming depleted in terms of non-disabled men. They were also overconfident, after having won victory after victory. So, they sent only a single regiment to Thrace to put down the insurrection. At Thrace, the Thracians and the Athenians employed mercenaries in their battle and surprised the Spartans. The Athenian and mercenaries used spears, knives, javelins, and shields. In Thrace, the Spartans were defeated and lost 250 more men.

BOETIAN WAR 378-371 BC

⚜

Thebes was the main city in the city-state of Boetia on the Eastern coast of the Southern Greek peninsula. Boetia had originally been a member of the Delian League, which had an agreement of mutual assistance in case of an attack. The war between Boetia and Thebes waged on and off for nearly ten years. King Aegisthus had led a force into Thebes earlier and won. However, the tide was turning. Sparta had been engaging in frequent wars and losing lots of its warriors in the process. Therefore, they had to use less-experienced soldiers in part of their formations. In 376 BC, the co-king, Cleombrotus, failed to make the perilous crossing at the Cithaeron Mountains, but the Athenians were able to do so.

⚜

In 375, King Cleombrotus altered his strategy and dispatched a naval force. However, Athens was already restoring its own navy and sent out a swift fleet to meet the Spartan vessels even before their arrival. The Athenians overcame the Spartans at sea under General Chabrias. Chabrias then laid siege to Spartan territories inside the province of Laconia.

BATTLE OF LEUCTRA

❦

By the year 371 BC, the Athenians and their allies were becoming more familiar with Sparta's traditional formations and battlefield techniques. At Leuctra, Spartans set up their phalanxes so that the more experienced warriors were at the right under King Cleombrotus and the least experienced at the left. This formation had become too predictable, so General Epaminondas of the Thebans attacked Sparta's weaker flank first. Instead of attacking with his full force all at once, Epaminondas staggered his flanks in order to weaken the advance force of Spartans. This break with tradition threw the Spartans into disarray, and they had to reformat themselves into an extended line rather than the tightly knit phalanx they preferred. This movement of men caused further confusion among the Spartan warriors. Taking advantage of that, the Athenians and Thebans defeated Sparta which sustained a heavy loss of men. Even King Cleombrotus himself was slain. The Boetian League with its

Thebans and Athenians had won. Sparta lost thousands of men, while the Boetian League only lost a few hundred.

⊗

Sparta had now lost its reputation as an invincible force. By the year 371 BC, it was less feared by the armies of Greece. After this weakening of the Spartan empire, democracy was then restored to Athens.

PLATO AND THE ATHENS
ACADEMY

❧

Plato, like his mentor, Socrates, devoted his life to higher learning. Plato's specialty was philosophy, and he educated his students in the kind of reasoning that would enhance their sense of justice and goodness. That, he felt, would yield a society in which would foster the search for ultimate truth by the people of Athens, and indeed that world beyond. His academy curriculum consisted of political philosophy, science, mathematics, spirituality, and ethics. The outcome of this education would not only yield intellectuals, but those intellectuals would produce societies that weren't embroiled in pettiness, greed, injustice and the kind of decadence that could destroy it. Plato contrasted two kinds of justice – that of the state and that of the truly just man.

❧

There is no record of the date of the construction of the Athens Academy, but archeologists had excavated a possible site outside the city of Athens. That site has within it a grove of olive trees, and narrations tell stories about students sitting with their teachers inside these olive orchards, enjoying the gentle wispy breezes, and in this natural setting, the students analyzed aspects of the world outside of them but especially explored the vistas of their own minds. Some have projected the actual founding of the school around 380 BC, and it continued under a succession of heads until 86 BC, when it was destroyed by the Roman tyrant Sulla after Rome conquered Greece.

THE ALLEGORY OF THE CAVE

The Allegory of the Cave was introduced in Plato's grand essay, the **Republic**. The Republic was an effort to explain how people perceive. Its final objective is to arrive as close to the truth as one can. The allegory is a story of men trapped within a dark cave but move from that darkness into the light that lies within their hearts and minds. The **Republic** highlights the manner in which a person can find the light:

> *"This very thing, then, I said, there might be an art, an art of the speediest and most effective shifting or conversion of the soul...toward the things that are real and true."*

Plato's objective was to train the leaders of tomorrow. Leaders were needed not only in government but among the leaders in mathematics, the science, literature, and art. If leaders in the future were virtuous, it would yield an enlightened society, and its legacy would last for generations to follow. History has proven that he was right.

❧ IV ❧
THE PERSIANS

One of the greatest empires of the ancient world was initiated by Alexander the Great. He was a student of Plato's Academy, under Aristotle – Plato's personal student. In many ways, he was the product of a new enlightened era of scholarship. However, as with most kings, he yielded to the temptation of expansion and conquest. He was a masterful ruler and a charismatic king but succumbed to the loss of virtue that all over-ambitious leaders fall prey to – blind and bloodthirsty greed for power. Those pseudo-emperors, however, serve a role in history by uniting small countries into a whole. Alexander, though, never lost his interest in promoting literature, art, philosophy, and medicine.

What had never been lost during his realm of service was the Grecian love of the arts and scholarship. A sign of respect for philosophy and the higher sciences flourished under Alexander in the areas of his territory that were stable.

ALEXANDER THE GREAT
336-323 BC

۞

After much had happened in Peloponnese and Southern Greece, especially in Sparta and Athens, Macedon was growing in strength. Macedon is located on the Northeastern area of the Greek peninsula. Kings there were very effective administrators and warriors. Kings Philip I and II had ruled there.

۞

Alexander was born in 356 BC to King Philip II. Great kings are always revered as being part divine in order to fortify the people's faith and loyalty. It was said that Alexander, then, was the son of the great god, **Zeus**.

EARLY MILITARY CAREER

hebes on the Eastern coast of Southern Greece had waged war with their Athenian allies against the ferocious Spartans during earlier classical times. In 338 BC, they confronted the mighty power of Macedon. Alexander fought for his father, King Philip II on behalf of Macedon.

BATTLE OF CHAERONEA 338 BC

A thens and Thebes had been growing in power, and themselves desired expansion into the Northeastern territory of Macedon. Inflated with the success of their campaigns which led to the fall the Spartan empire, Athens and Thebes of the province of Boetia on the lower peninsula boldly took on the great Macedonian armies under Alexander. At Chaeronea on the Northern border of Boetia, Philip and Alexander's stratagem of battle formations altered during the middle of the battle, but it was highly complex. The Athenian-Theban enemies maintained their tried and true practices of straight line formations, while the Macedonians exercised a circling maneuver. That surprised the Athenian and Theban legions and their men went into disarray. While the Delian League had masterful cavalry forces, Alexander's steed, Bucephalus, and the other muscular horses of the Macedonian's light and heavy cavalry stole the day.

The Thebans and Athenians had the reputation of being the finest fighting force in Greece, but it was destroyed in this day-long bloody encounter. Thousands of bloodies corpses were strewn across the battlefield, come twilight. In the end, there were around 3,000 Athenian and Theban warriors lying dead on the plains near the sea.

GENERAL ANTIPATER AND THE ANGRY ATHENIANS

Antipater became Alexander's loyal subject and general – forever faithful to the imperialistic desires of the great territory of Macedonia. He served as an ambassador to Athens following their defeat in that Battle of Chaeronea and negotiated peace. His son, Cassander, later came to the aid of the Athenians after he became an interim head of the Macedonian Empire.

THE TREATY OF COMMON PEACE
IN 338 BC

෴

Found in an ancient inscription in Athens, fragments of that peace treaty signed by Alexander, was preserved by archeologists. In part, it says:

> *"Oath. I swear by Zeus, Geia, Helios, Poseidon and all the gods and goddesses that I will abide by a common peach and will neither break nor harbor by craft or contrivance, with the intent of war against the participants of the war. Nor shall I depose the kindship of Philip or his descendants, nor the constitutions existing in each state, when they swore the oaths of peace."*

෴

This treaty was proposed to the League of Corinth, which was a league of smaller city-states, of which Thebes was the most dominant member. Stubborn Sparta, which hadn't joined that league, was coerced into doing so after Philip and Alexander's impressive victory at Chaeronea.

※

Alexander appreciated the militaristic attitude of the Spartans but disliked the democracy of Athens. When he and his father, Philip I, took over Athens, democracy was abolished.

※

Antipater was then entrusted with the sacred duty of heading the Macedonians after Alexander moved Eastward into Anatolia and Asia Minor.

※

It was Antipater's responsibility now to shore up the city-states of the lower Greek peninsula and place them under Macedonian control. Many of those city-states had joined the League of Corinth, and his response was to quell rebellions and resistance to the rule of Macedon.

※

The League of Corinth was later known as the Hellenic League under Alexander.

ACCESSION OF ALEXANDER THE GREAT

Alexander rose to the throne in 336 BC after the assassination of his father, Philip. The assassination was always a threat to a king and emperor by dangerous and jealous under-lords of lesser kingdoms. From ancient times and up into the Middle Ages, this was a frequent way used to seize a throne.

CAMPAIGN INTO ANATOLIA AND PHOENICIA

⁂

In Anatolia, King Darius III had grown confident since the Persian conquests under his predecessors, Darius I and Darius II. Persia was extremely wealthy in resources and was on the trade routes from the Near and Far East. The treasures brought back from that trade supplied its military with the finances necessary to fashion highly-developed weaponry, military equipment and armor for infantry and cavalry of its soldiers.

⁂

Wealth, however, brought many drawbacks with it like luxuries and licentious living. Corruption often prevailed in many of these minor sub-kingdoms as well, which resulted in sluggishness. In addition, battle-weary warriors often grew tired and lax, due to the incessant demands placed upon them and their performance.

❧

Darius had such a dilemma facing him after so many engagements had happened, and he had lost so many men in battle. He was in perennial need of new recruits who weren't experienced in the tactics of the battle. That was the situation in Issus, a city in Southern Anatolia.

THE BATTLE OF ISSUS 333 BC

The Greeks under Alexander had rehearsed many techniques and discovered that the most effective way to beat the Persians was to break up their very long phalanxes, divide them and encircle one part their flank while routing the other flank. Unfortunately, the Persians used a similar tactic on the Greeks, and – for a while – were weakening. However, Alexander himself came to the rescue and devised a ruse. Darius' soldiers fell into disorder Persian and were retreating. Alexander then temporarily let them do so. Next, Alexander gathered up his Greek phalanxes to the left and rerouted them to chase after the Persians. Thus, Darius and the Persians were defeated, and many of those who weren't slain were taken into slavery. Alexander now had a foothold in Anatolia.

PEACE ATTEMPT

⸙

In the year 333 BC, Alexander sent a missive to King Darius III. He wanted to negotiate peace with the Persians if Darius would declare that Alexander was the **"King of Asia**." By agreeing to that, Darius would be spared the bloodshed of prolonging the long war. This proposal was like a two-edged sword, however, having contained within it overtures of peace, but threats and challenges as well. In the letter, Alexander said:

> *"You shall have whatever you persuade me to give. And in the future when you send to me, makes your addresses to the king of Asia, and do not correspond as an equal, but tell me, as lord of all your possessions, what you need; otherwise, I shall make plans to deal with you as a wrongdoer. But if you claim the kingship, stand your ground and fight for it, and do not flee, I shall pursue you wherever you are."*

The proposal wasn't accepted.

THE BATTLES OF TYRE AND
SIDON 332 BC

Tyre was in an enviable position on the Eastern Mediterranean and has long been known in song as a story as the most prominent city in Phoenicia. (current-day Syria) The Phoenicians were famous as masters of the sea. Their skills at shipbuilding had been honed for centuries. Alexander attempted to conquer Sidon and was successful there. However, that left Tyre. Tyre was on a small island just off the coast and was defended quite adequately by immense city walls and a formidable navy. Initially, Alexander wasn't able to conquer Tyre.

He then pulled back to the mainland and had his men build a causeway across the channel. At the end of the causeway, he erected siege engines to mount the city walls and have his foot soldiers raid the port city and allow for his infantry to enter. Simultaneously, he employed the services of Greek shipbuilders to build a large navy for him.

❧

With that navy, Alexander blocked the harbor and laid siege to Tyre, realizing that the men inside the city would run out of water, food, and supplies. In a message sent to the Tyrians, he promised amnesty to those who took sanctuary in the temple of Artemis, the goddess of the moon, the son and of children.

❧

After his navy arrived, Alexander's foot soldiers mounted the city walls and slaughtered many who were defending it. There were some naval skirmishes, but the Phoenician navy had been blocked from entry into Tyre by Alexander's fleet.

❧

As a result of his campaigns from Sidon and Tyre, Alexander conquered the Levant. The Levant, at that time, consisted of all the smaller provinces along the Eastern Mediterranean coast and Gaza which was the gateway to Egypt.

ALEXANDER THE GREAT
CONQUERS EGYPT

❦

Egypt had been a glorious kingdom, replete with culture and great stone pyramids. It was a land for the Egyptians who peacefully toiled the fertile valley of the Nile River. Frescoes, sculptures and beautiful representations of their deities adorned the villages and towns. However, when the Persians invaded Egypt, their rulers were no longer pharaohs like those of the Early and Middle Kingdom. Egypt was under the crushing oppression of foreigners. The Persians then became pharaohs. The Egyptian culture, the legacy of the great pharaohs like Tutankhamun and Rameses II thus faded into history.

❦

King Darius of the Persians had now assumed control of Egypt. However, in 332 BC, when Alexander arrived, he was greeted as a liberator by the rebellious Egyptians who despised the Persian rule. Alexander was paraded to their great capital of Memphis and crowned as pharaoh of upper and lower Egypt, and the Persians were exiled from the country by its own people. The city of Alexandria is named after Alexander the Great.

Under Alexander, the Egyptians felt they would no longer be suppressed by these foreigners from Asia Minor. Greece had been trading partners with Egypt for many centuries after that, and each culture appreciated the beauty of the others' accomplishments and culture.

ORACLE OF AMMON

※

mmon was a deity revered by the Egyptians and the Libyans alike, as the people of those two countries were of related tribes. When Alexander was in Egypt, he consulted with the Oracle of Ammon who was 300 west of Egypt at a place in the Western desert called the Siwa Oasis.

※

There Alexander was greeted by the temple priests, and they brought up a litter carrying the ram-headed god, **Ammon**. The idol was adorned with precious gems. His communications and the response of the oracle shall forever remain hidden from history; verbal reports passed along through the generations indicate that he "***received the answer his soul desired***," and he left with a smile on his face.

※

Alexander then pursued a course into Babylon, Asia Minor including Iran. He even went as far as India in the name of the Greek Empire of Macedonia.

DARIUS LOCATED!

☙❧

In Persia, Alexander found Darius at Ectabana, its main capital city. Ectabana is currently within the country of Iran. However, the great King Darius III was dead. He was assassinated by his men who wanted a man by the name of Bessus to rule in his stead. The body of the former King, Darius III, had been thrown into an ox cart. Alexander reverently removed it himself and gave King Darius a respectable burial.

DEATH OF ALEXANDER 323 BC

It was Alexander's dream to have people from all the races in the known world to unite together and dismiss their petty jealousies and squabbles. Toward that end, he held a huge banquet in the temple of the ancient Babylonian King, Nebuchadnezzar, and asked for them to unite together. Many objected, but Alexander reminded his regiments that he had marched them from victory to victory. Nevertheless, he gave them a choice to stay with him or leave. No one left.

At the celebration, it was reported by the ancient historians, Arrian and Diodorus, that he drank a libation of wine. However, later in the evening, he died. Word then went out that he was poisoned. Alexander was only 32-years old.

After Alexander's death, his successors lost full control over the Asian sector of his Macedonian kingdom. Between the years 312 BC and 63 BC, the territory of Anatolia, the Levant, Mesopotamia and area further east in Asia became the Seleucid Empire. They were succeeded by the Sasanian Dynasty out of Baghdad of current-day Iraq. When Alexander annexed Egypt, he had expanded the Persian territories Westward across the Maghreb of North Africa. The Maghreb was ruled by Ptolemy I of Egypt on behalf of the Greeks. Cultures of those two areas were vastly different, so a spit between them and Greece proper seems logical. The truly traditional Greek culture and people shrunk to center and rested mostly upon the provinces of mainland Greece and Peloponnese, who were all united by a root language. Some rulers died due to assassinations, and others were defeated in battle. The Persian Empire Alexander had created was too diverse and widely scattered to have lasted more than a few years.

THE HELLENISTIC LEAGUE

The Hellenistic League was formed from what had been known as the Achaean League in 280 BC. It was a confederation of the union of the Hellenistic dynasty of mainland Greece and the city-states of Peloponnese off Southern Greece's Western coast. The kings of the Hellenistic dynasty were descendants of Alexander the Great, even if distantly related. Portions of the Hellenistic League were still in the hands of those who were associated with Alexander, such as Cassander, who restored democracy to Athens.

During this period, Macedon went through a succession of leaders. By 245 BC, Athens had lost its democracy and independence. Thebes became the most powerful of the provinces in the Peloponnese, and the Achaean League was joined with the Hellenistic League. Despite the swapping of governmental powers and institutions, the Hellenistic era was a time that gave rise to a proliferation of philosophy, architecture, literature, and art. The beauty of the treasures the Hellenistic Greeks left behind draw people from all corners of the globe. In addition, every major and even minor museum has artifacts manifesting the glory of their accomplishments.

LAOCOON

০⁕৩

One of the most exquisite examples of the Hellenistic style was the multi-figured marble statues of Laocoon. Most Hellenistic art themes begin with the deity myths. In the ancient poet's epic, the **Aeneid**, it tells the story of a Trojan priest who tried to warn the Trojans that the wooden statue of the horse was hiding Greek warriors and he is punished for it, along with his sons. It was sculpted between the years 42-20 BC. The powerful sculpture is displayed in the Vatican museum.

VENUS DE MILO

Believed to have been carved around 120 BC, this famous statue portrays the deity, *Aphrodite*. It represents beauty in its perfection and the elegance of the human form. Its posture signifies dignity and eroticism, but one that radiates femininity.

ALEXANDER MOSAIC

৩৵৶

Very often scholars refer to paintings, frescoes, and mosaics to narrate their essays containing historical information. Although they aren't always absolutely accurate depictions, they do reveal details about battles and events not recorded in the ancient history texts. The Alexander mosaic completed around 100 BC is modeled after a painting by Philoxenus of Eretria off the East coast of Southern Greece. The painting was done for King Cassander of Macedon (see earlier).

৩৵৶

It depicts the Battle of Issus of 333 BC against King Darius III.

PRELUDE TO THE INVASION OF ROME

After the death of Alexander the Great, the kingdoms of the Empire of Greece were subdivided by the military generals – Antipater being the first. (see earlier) Simultaneously, Rome was rising as the next imperial domineering power. Rome achieved its entrance to Greece and the world lying east of there after they conquered the might power of Carthage in Maghreb. Carthage had been the formidable ruler of the Mediterranean Sea. Hannibal was from Carthage and had the same ambition as Rome – that is, to conquer and subdue the countries in Italy and East.

Hannibal took on Greece directly by going to war with Macedon and engaging Greece in a 20-year war. The Seleucid Empire (the Persians) were defeated by Rome at the Greek city of Thermopylae. With the victory, the Roman Empire needed to subdue Greece, except for the stubborn city of Corinth. In 146 BC, the Achaean League rebelled against the Roman consular control under Mummius.

THE BATTLE OF CORINTH 146 BC

Initially, in this battle, the Achaeans won the first engagement. Once they had defeated the Roman legions, they thought the encounter was over. However, they underestimated the superior military strategy so typical of Rome and hadn't prepared themselves for the counter-attack that followed. When they had sufficient numbers and outnumbered the enemy, Rome often charged full-flank into an enemy. This they did at Corinth, and the Greeks were roundly defeated.

That marked the end of Hellenistic Greece.

GRECO-ROMAN AND BYZANTINE GREECE

However, when the Romans were exposed to the magnificence of Greek literature, architecture, and art, they stood in such great admiration of it to the point that Roman artisans and scholars combined the two cultures. The Hellenistic influence is evident in the art of Ancient Rome. According to the poet, Horace,

"Captive Greece took captive her savage conqueror."

GRECO-ROMAN PERIOD 146 BC-394 AD

*A*fter the Battle of Corinth, Greece became a Roman protectorate. To weaken the powerful leagues like the Achaean or Hellenistic League and city-states, the Romans divided Greece into provinces:

- Achaea
- Macedonia
- Epirus
- Thrace
- Moesia
- The Achaean Islands

The Greek language became the predominant language of the Eastern Mediterranean World. A non-Greek wasn't considered educated unless he spoke Greek. It was the language of the finest literature in the known world. It was the language of the scholars and was used in the institutes of higher learning. In fact, many of the original manuscripts that were contained in the Christian Bible were written in Greek. The word "***barbarian***" originally referred to someone who didn't speak Greek.

◈

The Roman nobles studied the philosophy of Socrates, Plato, and Aristotle. Those Romans who could afford it, went to Greece to study and to watch its charioteer races and the Olympics.

◈

The Roman deities were increased to incorporate some of the Greek deities, and **"*mystery religions*"** were adopted by practitioners from around the Roman empire. Particular fascinating was a belief entitled the Eleusinian Mysteries.

ELEUSINIAN MYSTERIES

❧

Belief in deities flowed from the belief that gods influence man in his undertakings in life. They tend to surround the importance of the seasons, as the proper sowing and harvesting of crops were essential to life.

❧

Ceres (also known as "***Demeter***") was the goddess of grain. *Ceres* had a daughter named **Persephone**. According to the legend, **Persephone** dwelt in the city of Eleusis near Athens. Religious festivals were held to celebrate the sowing and reaping of grain, and the rites were enacted in the Greek cities. These celebrations were ways in which the people paid homage to the gods in order to obtain their favor and blessings for health the prosperity.

THE LEGEND OF PERSEPHONE

ॐ

This myth was the allegorical re-telling of the cycle of death and rebirth, and the cycle of death and rebirth is one that is a tenet of the world's greatest religions. As the tale relates, it was said the god of the underworld, **Hades**, wanted a wife and kidnapped **Persephone**, dragging her down to the netherworld. Because **Persephone** was taken, **Ceres**, her mother was so distraught that she didn't tend to her godly duties involving the harvest, and the grain didn't grow. It wasn't until a compromise could be reached that the harvest could be plentiful. The compromise called for **Hades** to permit **Persephone** to visit her mother, **Ceres**, that the harvest could be fruitful.

That myth revealed the cycle of growth – from seeding to growth to harvest and then followed by a period of rest. Thus, the seasons were explained. The same cycle was used to

146

elucidate the mystery of life − from birth to death and resurrection or rebirth. The message of Eleusis was that − out of death comes a glorious rebirth into immortality.

BYZANTINE GREECE 394-600 AD

❧

In the late 4th Century, the Roman Empire was invaded by a succession of Germanic and Eastern tribes. It was first triggered by the invasion of Attila the Hun. The populations of the Northern regions of Europe and the Eastern Slavic nations had increased to the point that the people needed to relocate and make settlements elsewhere. Greece and Rome were warmer regions that were more fertile than the lands occupied by the Germanic tribes, and they craved the warmth and bounty of the fields that bordered the great Mediterranean Sea. The last emperor of Rome, a young boy by the auspicious name of Romulus, was defeated by Odoacer of the Ostrogoths, a nomadic tribe in 476 AD. That signaled the final end of the Roman empire.

❧

Gradually, the pagan religions of Ancient Greece were giving way to the new religion, Christianity. Christianity came to the forefront under Emperor Constantine the Great. Constantine was the son of a Roman general, and his mother was Helena the Greek. Even most of the Germanic tribes, including Odoacer who conquered Rome, had converted to Christianity. Within Constantine was a hereditary fusion of both Rome and Greece. Constantine's successor, Emperor Theodosius, established the Christian religion as the mandated religion of the Mediterranean World. In 364 AD the Empire was split into two divisions – the Western Roman Empire and the Byzantine Empire in the East. Greece was within the Byzantine region.

EMPEROR JUSTINIAN AND THE GREEKS

☙❧

Justinian had succeeded as Emperor of Byzantine Empire in the year 565 AD. His obsession included the regulation of every facet of people's lives and that included the people of Greece. As Christianity was the established religion, toleration of other sects, including that of the Greek and Roman deities was forbidden. Those who practiced pagan religions were persecuted. Many of the institutions of the magnificent Hellenistic and earlier traditions were destroyed. That included the Athens Academy started by Plato. Worship at the Siwa Oasis, where Alexander the Great met with the Oracle of Ammon, was abolished.

☙❧

The capital of the Byzantine Empire was Constantinople, named after Emperor Constantine. It was in the former city of Istanbul in Anatolia.

Regardless of the mandated religion of Christianity and Justinian's intrusion into the sacred sects of the Greeks, Greek artisans, architect's and learned scholars were always highly respected. They were drafted to render their services to the Byzantine Empire.

ISIDORE OF MILETUS

Isidore was a Greek mathematician and architect. In the year 532 AD, he and Anthemius of Tralles, who was also a Greek, were selected to redesign and rebuild the Hagia Sophia, a cathedral in Constantinople. It had been destroyed by a massive riot in the city. The Hagia Sophia was by far the largest structure of its kind in the known world. It incorporates the style of the long hallway of a Roman basilica combined with a magnificent dome in the center.

JUSTINIAN'S PLAGUE CIRCA 541-600 AD

᚛❧᚜

Probably brought into Constantinople in 541 AD, the bacterium that caused the outbreak of "***Justinian's Plague***" was transported in grain shipments from Egypt. Its origin is from a flea that infests rats, and these rats were often transported along with the grain they feed upon. The bacterium was the ***Yersinia pestis***, the same bacterium that causes the bubonic plague. It is the first pandemic ever recorded in history. Although exact numbers aren't known today, it was said that nearly 40% of the population had been destroyed by Justinian's plague. This bacterium raged throughout the known world and reoccurred in certain regions throughout the years. It was the precursor of that is known as the "***Black Death***" of the 13th Century.

❧ VI ❧
CONCLUSION

※

From Greece came the great conqueror of the Mediterranean World, Alexander the Great, and the world's philosophers like Socrates and Plato. Greek religions, although paganistic, reveal some of the very mysteries of life itself such as rebirth after death. Scientists measured the circumference of the earth from the grassy plains. The great city-states of Ancient Greece, Sparta and Athens have inspired the models for warfare and the rationale behind democratic institutions.

※

Greece rendered the classics and poetry of literature. Their scientists explored the areas of psychology, geometry, physics, political science, mathematics, and even medicine. Greek philosophy is studied today and gave rise to many new philosophies.

❦ VII ❧
FURTHER READING

❦

- Boardman, J. (1989) *Greek Art* Thames and Hudson
- Burn, L. (2005) *Hellenistic Art: From Alexander the Great to Augustus* J. Paul Getty Trust Publications
- Charbonneaux, J., Martin, J. & Villard, R. (1973) *Hellenistic Greece* Braziller
- Gouvousis, N. (1995) *Acropolis of Athens* Athens Publications
- Hall, J. J. (ed) (2014) *A History of the Archaic Greek World ca. 1200-479 BCE* Wiley-Blackwell
- Goldsmith, O. (1812) *The History of Greece, from the Earliest State, to the Death of Alexander the Great* University of Toronto Press
- Herodotus & Taylor, I. (ed) (1829) *Herodotus* The British Library

- Homer, and Fagles, R. (trans) (1990) *The Iliad* Penguin Putnam

YOUR FREE EBOOK!

As a way of saying thank you for reading our book, we're offering you a free copy of the below eBook.

Happy Reading!

GO WWW.THEHISTORYHOUR.COM/CLEO/

www.ingramcontent.com/pod-product-compliance
Lightning Source LLC
Chambersburg PA
CBHW031118250726
48655CB00004B/1756

9 781791 991623